# The Landlord's Mortgage Handbook: Navigating Buy to Let in the UK

Mark Parry

Mark Parry

Copyright © 2024 Mark Parry.

All rights reserved.

No part of this book may be reproduced, or stored in a retrieval system, or transmitted in any form or by any means, electronic, mechanical, photocopying, recording, or otherwise, without express written permission of the publisher.

ISBN: 9798342681162

Cover design by: Mark Parry

## Table Of Contents

Chapter 1: Introduction to Buy to Let Mortgages

Chapter 2: The Buy to Let Market in the UK

Chapter 3: Types of Buy to Let Mortgages

Chapter 4: Eligibility Criteria for Buy to Let Mortgages

Chapter 5: The Application Process

Chapter 6: Understanding Mortgage Terms

Chapter 7: Choosing the Right Lender

Chapter 8: Managing Your Buy to Let Property

Chapter 9: Tax Implications for Landlords

Chapter 10: Refinancing Your Buy to Let Mortgage

Chapter 11: Future Trends in Buy to Let

Chapter 12: Conclusion

# Chapter 1: Introduction to Buy to Let Mortgages

**Understanding Buy to Let**

Understanding Buy to Let involves grasping the fundamental principles behind this investment strategy, which entails purchasing residential properties with the primary intention of renting them out. This approach has gained significant popularity in the UK as a means of generating passive income and building wealth over time. While it may seem straightforward, prospective investors must navigate a range of considerations, from property selection to financial implications, to ensure the success of their buy-to-let ventures.

The first step in the buy-to-let process is identifying the right property. Location plays a critical role in this decision, as properties in areas with high rental demand tend to yield better returns.

Factors such as proximity to transport links, schools, and amenities can significantly affect a property's desirability. Investors should conduct thorough market research, analysing local rental prices and vacancy rates, to make informed choices that align with their investment goals.

Once a suitable property is identified, the next crucial aspect is securing financing through a buy-to-let mortgage. Unlike standard residential mortgages, buy-to-let mortgages consider the potential rental income as part of the application process. Lenders typically require a larger deposit—often at least 25% of the property's value—and may apply stricter affordability criteria. Understanding the various types of buy-to-let mortgages available, including fixed-rate and variable-rate options, is essential for investors to select the best financing solution for their circumstances.

In addition to financing, investors must also be aware of the ongoing costs associated with buy-to-let properties. These can include property management fees, maintenance costs, insurance, and, importantly, mortgage interest payments.

It is vital to create a comprehensive budget that accounts for these expenses to ensure that rental income can cover costs and still provide a profit.

Understanding tax implications, such as the treatment of rental income and allowable expenses, is also crucial for financial planning and compliance with UK tax laws.

Finally, successful buy-to-let investment requires adopting a proactive approach to property management. This encompasses understanding tenant rights, ensuring properties meet safety and habitability standards, and maintaining open communication with tenants. Building a positive landlord-tenant relationship can lead to higher tenant retention rates and reduced vacancy periods. As the buy-to-let landscape continues to evolve, staying informed about regulatory changes and market trends will empower landlords to make strategic decisions that enhance their investment portfolio's performance.

## Benefits of Buy to Let Mortgages

Buy to let mortgages offer a range of benefits that can significantly enhance a property investor's portfolio. One of the primary advantages is the potential for generating a steady stream of rental income.

By acquiring properties specifically for rental purposes, landlords can create a reliable cash flow that can help cover mortgage payments and other associated costs. This income can be particularly advantageous in offsetting expenses and contributing to overall financial stability, making it a compelling option for investors looking to diversify their income sources.

Another key benefit of buy to let mortgages is the opportunity for capital appreciation. Over time, property values tend to increase, which can lead to substantial returns on investment. By leveraging a buy to let mortgage, investors can purchase properties without needing to pay the full purchase price upfront. This allows them to benefit from property value increases while only having a portion of their own capital tied up in the investment.

As property values rise, landlords can realise significant profits when selling the property or can choose to refinance to access equity for further investments.

Tax advantages also play a significant role in the attractiveness of buy to let mortgages.

Landlords can often deduct various expenses related to property management, including mortgage interest, maintenance costs, and property management fees, from their taxable income. This can lower the overall tax burden and improve the investment's profitability. Additionally, with recent changes in tax legislation, landlords must stay informed about regulations that may impact their financial responsibilities, but the potential for tax relief remains a crucial factor in many investors' decision-making processes.

Buy to let mortgages also provide investors with the opportunity to build equity over time. As tenants pay rent, landlords gradually pay down the mortgage principal, which increases their equity stake in the property. This growing equity can serve as a financial resource for future investments, allowing landlords to reinvest in their portfolios or finance additional properties.

Furthermore, building equity can enhance long-term financial security, as it provides a buffer against market fluctuations and the potential for future cash flow.

Finally, investing in buy to let properties can foster a sense of community and contribute positively to local economies.

Landlords play a vital role in providing housing options, which can help meet demand in areas with limited rental availability. This not only supports the housing market but can also lead to improved property values in the surrounding area. By participating in the buy to let market, investors can make a meaningful impact while also reaping the financial benefits that come from successful property investment strategies.

**Risks Involved**

In the realm of buy to let investments, landlords must navigate a landscape fraught with various risks that can significantly impact their financial returns. Understanding these risks is crucial for making informed decisions. One of the primary risks is market fluctuation. Property values can rise and fall due to economic conditions, changes in the housing market, or shifts in demand.

A decline in property prices can not only affect the ability to sell the property at a profit but can also impact the value of the property as collateral for the mortgage. Landlords should conduct thorough market research and keep abreast of trends to mitigate this risk.

Another significant risk involves tenant management. The potential for having problematic tenants can lead to a host of challenges, including late rent payments, property damage, or even legal disputes. These issues can result in unexpected costs and can disrupt cash flow, making it essential for landlords to employ effective tenant screening processes. A well-structured tenancy agreement can also serve as a protective measure, clearly outlining the expectations and responsibilities of both parties.

Vacancy rates pose another risk that landlords must consider. Periods without a tenant can lead to a loss of rental income, which can severely affect the financial viability of a buy to let investment. Factors contributing to vacancy rates can include economic downturns, seasonal demand fluctuations, or even property location.

To reduce this risk, landlords should ensure their properties are well-maintained and competitively priced, and they may also consider employing professional letting agents to enhance marketing efforts and tenant acquisition strategies.

Regulatory changes also represent a significant risk in the buy to let sector. The UK government frequently updates legislation affecting landlords, such as changes to tax relief, energy efficiency requirements, and eviction processes. Staying compliant with these regulations is essential to avoid fines and legal complications. Landlords should remain informed about current laws and consider consulting with legal professionals to ensure they understand their obligations and the potential implications of any regulatory changes on their investment.

Lastly, financial risks cannot be overlooked. Changes in interest rates can impact mortgage repayments and overall profitability. If a landlord is on a variable-rate mortgage, rising interest rates could lead to increased monthly payments, squeezing profit margins. Additionally, unforeseen expenses such as maintenance and repairs can arise, leading to budget overruns.

Landlords should plan for such contingencies by maintaining an emergency fund and considering fixed-rate mortgages to lock in current rates and provide a degree of financial certainty.

By understanding and preparing for these risks, landlords can enhance their chances of success in the buy to let market.

# Chapter 2: The Buy to Let Market in the UK

### Overview of the UK Property Market

The UK property market is a dynamic landscape that has undergone significant transformations over the years, shaped by various economic, social, and political factors. As of 2024, the property market continues to exhibit resilience despite challenges such as inflation and changes in government policies. For investors considering buy-to-let opportunities, understanding the nuances of the current market is crucial for making informed decisions. This overview aims to shed light on key trends, regional variations, and the overall climate affecting landlords and property investors.

One notable trend in the UK property market is the continued demand for rental properties, particularly in urban areas. Cities such as London, Manchester, and Birmingham have seen substantial population growth, fuelling the need for more housing.

The increasing difficulty for first-time buyers to enter the property market has led to a growing pool of potential tenants. This demand creates opportunities for buy-to-let investors, who can benefit from stable rental income and potential capital appreciation. However, prospective landlords must remain vigilant about local market conditions, as demand can vary significantly from one region to another.

Another important aspect of the UK property market is the impact of government regulations and policies on landlords. Recent years have seen a tightening of regulations aimed at ensuring tenant protections and promoting responsible renting. Measures such as the introduction of minimum energy efficiency standards and the potential for rent controls in certain areas may influence investment decisions. Landlords need to stay informed about these changes, as compliance can affect profitability and operational strategies. Understanding the regulatory landscape is essential for mitigating risks associated with property investment.

Financing options for buy-to-let properties have also evolved, influenced by economic conditions and lending practices.

Buy-to-let mortgages remain a popular choice for investors, offering various products tailored to different circumstances. Lenders typically assess the rental income potential of a property, requiring a thorough understanding of rental yields and market rates. Investors should carefully evaluate mortgage products, interest rates, and terms to ensure they choose the best financing strategy for their portfolio. The interplay between interest rates and property prices can significantly impact investment returns, making it essential to approach financing with a strategic mindset.

Finally, prospects for the UK property market remain a subject of keen interest. While uncertainties such as economic fluctuations and potential changes in government leadership can create volatility, many analysts remain optimistic about long-term growth in the housing sector. As remote working trends continue to influence where people choose to live, suburban and rural areas may see increased demand, presenting new opportunities for buy-to-let investors. Understanding these trends, along with ongoing market analysis, will be vital for landlords aiming to navigate the complexities of the UK property market successfully.

## Trends and Forecasts

The buy-to-let market in the UK has experienced significant fluctuations over the past decade, influenced by various economic factors, regulatory changes, and shifting consumer preferences. One of the key trends observed is the increasing demand for rental properties, particularly in urban areas. As more individuals opt for flexibility over homeownership, cities like London, Manchester, and Birmingham have seen a surge in tenant populations. This trend suggests that landlords can expect a sustained interest in rental accommodations, making buy-to-let investments a potentially lucrative opportunity in the near future.

Alongside the demand for rental properties, the rental price growth has been a notable trend. Despite periodic economic challenges, rental prices in many regions have continued to rise, driven by factors such as limited housing supply, increasing construction costs, and heightened competition among tenants. This upward trajectory in rental prices indicates that landlords can anticipate a favourable return on investment.

However, it is crucial for landlords to remain vigilant about market conditions and regional variations, as these can significantly impact rental yields.

In terms of financing, the landscape of buy-to-let mortgages in the UK is evolving. Lenders are increasingly offering more diverse mortgage products tailored to the unique needs of landlords. For instance, there has been a rise in specialist buy-to-let mortgages that cater to portfolio landlords, allowing for greater flexibility in managing multiple properties. Furthermore, the advent of technology has streamlined the mortgage application process, enabling landlords to access financing more efficiently. As the market continues to mature, landlords may find more innovative financial solutions becoming available.

Regulatory changes also play a critical role in shaping the future of the buy-to-let market. Recent government initiatives aimed at improving housing standards and tenant protections have introduced new compliance requirements for landlords.

While these regulations are designed to enhance tenant welfare, they also necessitate that landlords stay informed and adapt their strategies accordingly. As the regulatory environment evolves, landlords who proactively embrace compliance will not only mitigate risks but also enhance their reputation and tenant relationships.

Looking ahead, forecasts for the buy-to-let sector suggest a cautious but optimistic outlook. Economic indicators, such as employment rates and consumer confidence, will continue to influence the rental market dynamics. Moreover, the increasing focus on sustainability and energy efficiency in housing may create new opportunities for landlords who invest in eco-friendly properties. Overall, by staying attuned to these trends and forecasts, landlords can navigate the complexities of the buy-to-let landscape more effectively and position themselves for long-term success.

**Regional Considerations**

When considering buy to let investments in the UK, regional variations play a crucial role in determining the potential success of a property venture.

Each region exhibits distinct market dynamics influenced by local economic conditions, demographic trends, and housing supply. Understanding these regional considerations can guide landlords in making informed decisions regarding property acquisition and management. For instance, areas with a strong rental demand, such as urban centres or university towns, often present more lucrative opportunities compared to rural regions with limited tenant demand.

The North-South divide is a prominent factor in the UK property market. The South, particularly London and the Southeast, has historically commanded higher property prices and rental yields. However, the North has seen significant growth in rental demand, driven by affordable housing and regeneration projects in cities like Manchester, Liverpool, and Leeds. Landlords must assess their investment goals and consider whether they prefer the higher costs and potentially lower yields of Southern properties or the more affordable options with higher yields in Northern regions.

Additionally, local government policies and planning regulations can significantly impact buy to let investments. Different local authorities have varying approaches to housing development, tenant rights, and licensing requirements. Regions with supportive policies for landlords may provide a more favourable environment for buy to let investments, while those with stringent regulations could pose challenges. It is essential for landlords to stay informed about the local legislative landscape and any upcoming changes that could affect their investments.

Economic factors, such as employment rates and average income levels, also vary by region and can influence tenant demand. Areas with growing job opportunities and increasing wages tend to attract more renters, contributing to a stable rental market. Conversely, regions experiencing economic decline may see reduced demand, leading to longer vacancy periods and lower rental income. Conducting thorough market research and analysis of economic indicators can help landlords identify promising regions for investment.

Finally, the impact of infrastructure developments cannot be understated. Major transport links, new schools, and healthcare facilities can enhance an area's attractiveness, driving up property values and rental demand. Landlords should pay attention to planned developments in their target regions, as these can signal future growth and increased tenant interest. By assessing regional considerations, landlords can strategically position themselves to maximise their buy to let investments across the diverse UK property landscape.

# Chapter 3: Types of Buy to Let Mortgages

**Standard Buy to Let Mortgages**

Standard buy to let mortgages are a popular choice for investors looking to enter the rental market in the UK. These mortgages are specifically designed for properties that will be rented out to tenants, as opposed to being occupied by the owner. The main feature of a standard buy to let mortgage is that it allows landlords to borrow against the value of the property they intend to rent, with repayment structures typically based on rental income. This type of mortgage can provide a reliable means of financing investment properties, given that the rental income is expected to cover mortgage repayments and other associated costs.

One of the key aspects of standard buy to let mortgages is the assessment process that lenders use to determine eligibility.

Unlike residential mortgages, which primarily consider the borrower's income, buy to let mortgages focus on the potential rental income of the property. Lenders require that the rental income covers a certain percentage of the mortgage payments, often around 125 to 145 percent, to ensure that the landlord can manage their financial obligations even if there are void periods or unexpected expenses. Additionally, lenders will evaluate the property's location, condition, and market demand, as these factors can significantly influence rental yields.

The deposit requirements for standard buy to let mortgages typically differ from those of residential mortgages. Most lenders will ask for a minimum deposit of 25 percent, although some may offer products with lower deposits available. A higher deposit can often lead to better interest rates, which can enhance the overall profitability of the investment. It is crucial for prospective landlords to consider their financial position and the potential impact of deposit size on cash flow and overall returns when selecting a mortgage product.

Interest rates on standard buy to let mortgages can vary significantly based on market conditions, the lender, and the borrower's financial profile.

Fixed-rate mortgages provide stability by locking in an interest rate for a predetermined period, while variable-rate mortgages can fluctuate based on changes in the Bank of England base rate. Investors should weigh the benefits of each type against their investment strategy and risk tolerance. Consulting with a mortgage advisor can be beneficial in navigating these options to find the most suitable product for individual circumstances.

Finally, it is essential for landlords to remain aware of the regulatory landscape affecting buy to let mortgages. Changes in tax legislation, such as the reduction of mortgage interest relief, can impact the profitability of rental properties. Landlords must also consider the implications of recent regulatory changes related to tenant safety and property standards. Staying informed about these factors is crucial for making sound investment decisions and ensuring compliance with legal requirements.

By understanding the intricacies of standard buy to let mortgages, landlords can better position themselves for success in the rental market.

**Limited Company Buy to Let Mortgages**

Limited company buy to let mortgages have gained increasing popularity among property investors in the UK, particularly considering recent tax changes and regulatory developments. These mortgages allow individuals to purchase rental properties through a limited company structure, which can offer distinct financial advantages. By using a limited company, landlords may be able to mitigate their personal tax liabilities, as profits generated from the rental income are taxed at the corporate tax rate, which is often lower than the higher rates of personal income tax.

One of the primary benefits of a limited company buy to let mortgage is the ability to offset mortgage interest payments against rental income before calculating tax. This is a significant advantage compared to individual landlords, who have faced restrictions on their mortgage interest tax relief since 2017.

As a result, many property investors have shifted to a limited company model to take advantage of this tax efficiency.

This shift could lead to increased net income, making property investment more appealing, particularly for those with multiple properties.

However, securing a limited company buy to let mortgage can be more complex than obtaining a standard residential buy to let mortgage. Lenders typically require additional documentation when considering applications from limited companies, including company accounts, business plans, and details about the directors and shareholders. The financial health of the company is scrutinised closely, as lenders want to ensure that the company has sufficient cash flow to cover mortgage repayments. Consequently, it is essential for potential investors to prepare thoroughly and provide comprehensive information to improve their chances of approval.

Furthermore, interest rates for limited company buy to let mortgages can sometimes be higher than those available to individual landlords. This discrepancy arises from the perceived risk associated with lending to a limited company structure.

Investors should take this into account when calculating potential returns on their investment. It is also important for landlords to shop around and compare offers from different lenders, as terms and conditions can vary significantly. Engaging with a mortgage broker who specialises in buy to let mortgages can provide invaluable insights and help navigate the complexities of the borrowing process.

In conclusion, limited company buy to let mortgages present a viable option for property investors looking to optimise their tax position and enhance their financial returns. While the application process may involve additional requirements and potential costs, the long-term benefits can outweigh these challenges. Landlords should consider their individual circumstances, investment goals, and financial strategies when deciding whether to pursue this route. As the buy to let landscape continues to evolve, understanding the nuances of limited company mortgages will be crucial for successful investment in the UK property market.

**Holiday Let Mortgages**

Holiday let mortgages have emerged as a popular option for property investors in the UK, particularly as the demand for short-term rental accommodations continues to grow. Unlike traditional buy-to-let mortgages, which are designed for long-term tenants, holiday let mortgages cater specifically to properties rented out on a short-term basis, typically for less than 30 days at a time. This subchapter will explore the unique features, requirements, and considerations associated with holiday let mortgages, providing valuable insights for landlords looking to diversify their portfolios.

One of the primary distinguishing features of holiday let mortgages is their lending criteria, which often differ significantly from standard buy-to-let mortgages. Lenders typically assess the property's potential rental income rather than relying solely on the borrower's personal income. This means that prospective borrowers must provide a detailed business plan, including projected rental income based on market analysis, occupancy rates, and seasonal variations.

It is crucial for landlords to conduct thorough research on their target market and to have realistic expectations regarding occupancy levels to secure the best mortgage terms available.

Additionally, many lenders require that holiday let properties meet certain criteria to qualify for a mortgage. For instance, the property must be situated in a suitable location for tourism, demonstrating potential for high occupancy rates. Furthermore, the property must be furnished and equipped for short-term stays, including amenities that cater to guests. Some lenders may also impose restrictions on the type of property eligible for a holiday let mortgage, focusing on residential properties rather than commercial or mixed-use buildings. Understanding these requirements is essential for landlords aiming to navigate the mortgage landscape effectively.

Another important consideration for landlords seeking holiday let mortgages is the tax implications associated with short-term rentals. The UK tax regime treats holiday lets differently than traditional buy-to-let properties.

Landlords may benefit from certain tax reliefs, such as the Furnished Holiday Let (FHL) rules, which allow for specific tax advantages, including capital allowances on furniture and fixtures. However, landlords must also be aware of the potential for additional tax responsibilities, such as VAT registration if the rental income exceeds a certain threshold. It is advisable for landlords to consult with tax professionals to ensure compliance and to maximise their financial benefits.

In conclusion, holiday let mortgages present a unique opportunity for property investors in the UK, allowing them to tap into the lucrative short-term rental market. By understanding the specific lending criteria, property requirements, and tax implications, landlords can make informed decisions when pursuing this type of mortgage. As the demand for holiday accommodations continues to rise, those who take the time to research and prepare will be well-positioned to capitalise on this growing trend in the real estate sector.

# Chapter 4: Eligibility Criteria for Buy to Let Mortgages

**Financial Requirements**

In the realm of buy-to-let investments, understanding the financial requirements is crucial for success. Prospective landlords must first consider the deposit needed for a buy-to-let mortgage, which typically ranges from 20% to 40% of the property's value. This initial investment not only demonstrates a commitment to the property but also impacts the overall mortgage terms and interest rates available. Lenders often favour larger deposits as they reduce the risk associated with the mortgage, potentially leading to more favourable borrowing conditions.

In addition to the deposit, landlords should be prepared for the associated costs of purchasing a property. These expenses can include stamp duty, legal fees, property surveys, and various administrative costs. Each of these elements can significantly affect the total financial outlay required to secure a buy-to-let property.

It is essential to budget for these costs alongside the purchase price to avoid any financial strain during the acquisition process.

Another significant financial consideration is the income generated from the rental property. Lenders typically require that rental income covers a certain percentage of the mortgage payment, often referred to as the "income coverage ratio." This ratio is crucial in determining the amount a landlord can borrow. Most lenders prefer a coverage ratio of around 125% to 145%, meaning that the expected rental income should be 125% to 145% of the monthly mortgage payment. This requirement ensures that landlords can manage their mortgage obligations even in the event of unexpected vacancies or maintenance costs.

Landlords must also account for additional financial responsibilities that come with property ownership. These include maintenance costs, property management fees, taxes, and insurance premiums. Setting aside a reserve fund for unexpected repairs and legal issues is a prudent strategy that can safeguard against financial difficulties.

Understanding these ongoing costs is vital for creating a realistic budget that aligns with the anticipated income from rental properties.

Finally, investors should consider the implications of interest rates on their financial planning. With fluctuating rates, the choice between fixed-rate and variable-rate mortgages can significantly impact monthly payments and overall investment profitability. A fixed-rate mortgage provides stability against rising interest rates, whereas a variable-rate mortgage may offer lower initial costs but comes with the risk of increasing payments. Engaging with a financial advisor or mortgage broker can provide tailored insights into navigating these complexities, ensuring that landlords make informed decisions that align with their financial goals in the buy-to-let market.

**Property Criteria**

When considering a buy to let investment, the selection of the property is paramount. Property criteria should encompass various aspects that influence both the immediate rental income and long-term capital appreciation.

Location remains one of the most critical factors; properties situated in areas with good transport links, local amenities, and reputable schools tend to attract higher demand from tenants. Researching areas with substantial rental yields and potential for growth is essential for ensuring that the investment remains viable over time.

Another key criterion is the type of property itself. Different types of properties, such as single-family homes, flats, or multi-units, will appeal to different demographics of tenants. For instance, families may prefer houses with gardens in suburban areas, while young professionals might be more interested in city-centre apartments. Understanding the target market and choosing properties that meet their needs can lead to lower vacancy rates and more consistent rental income. Furthermore, considering the property's condition and the potential need for renovation can significantly impact initial costs and ongoing maintenance.

Financial considerations also play a vital role in property selection. Investors should evaluate the purchase price in relation to the expected rental income to determine the property's yield.

A common benchmark is to aim for a gross rental yield of at least 6% to ensure the investment is worthwhile. Additionally, understanding the costs associated with property management, maintenance, and potential void periods is crucial to creating a comprehensive financial plan.

This analysis will help investors assess whether the investment aligns with their financial goals and risk tolerance.

Legal and regulatory factors must also be considered when selecting a property. Buy to let landlords in the UK must comply with various regulations, including safety standards, tenancy agreements, and licensing requirements. Properties located in areas with strict regulations may require additional investment in compliance measures. Familiarising oneself with local housing laws and understanding the implications of these regulations can prevent costly mistakes and ensure a smoother tenancy experience.

Lastly, the market conditions can significantly impact property criteria.

Staying informed about trends in the real estate market, such as changes in interest rates, demand fluctuations, and economic conditions, is essential for making informed investment decisions. Timing the market and understanding when to buy or sell properties can affect profitability. By carefully considering these property criteria, investors can position themselves for success in the competitive buy to let sector, ultimately leading to a profitable and sustainable rental business.

**Landlord Experience**

The landlord experience in the UK housing market is characterised by a blend of financial acumen, property management skills, and an understanding of tenant needs. Successful landlords recognise that their role extends beyond merely collecting rent; it involves actively managing properties, ensuring tenant satisfaction, and maintaining compliance with evolving regulations. A comprehensive approach to property management not only enhances tenant retention but also maximises returns on investment, making the buy-to-let journey more rewarding.

Navigating the complexities of buy-to-let mortgages is crucial for prospective landlords. The UK mortgage market offers a variety of products tailored specifically for landlords, each with its own requirements and implications. Understanding the differences between standard buy-to-let mortgages, limited company mortgages, and portfolio landlord mortgages is essential. Landlords must assess their financial situations and long-term goals to choose the most suitable mortgage product, as this decision can significantly impact cash flow and profitability.

Effective property management is a cornerstone of a positive landlord experience. This encompasses various responsibilities, including property maintenance, tenant communication, and legal compliance. Landlords should establish clear communication channels with tenants to address issues promptly and foster a positive living environment. Additionally, staying informed about legal obligations, such as those related to safety and tenant rights, is vital to avoiding potential disputes and ensuring a smooth tenancy.

Moreover, the importance of regular property maintenance cannot be overstated. A well-maintained property not only attracts quality tenants but also helps in retaining them. Routine inspections and timely repairs can prevent small issues from escalating into costly problems. Landlords should also consider investing in upgrades that enhance the property's appeal, such as energy-efficient appliances or modern fixtures, which can justify higher rental prices and increase overall property value.

Finally, networking, and continuous education play significant roles in enhancing the landlord experience. Engaging with other landlords, joining local property groups, or participating in online forums can provide valuable insights and advice. Additionally, staying updated on market trends, changes in legislation, and best practices can empower landlords to make informed decisions. By fostering a proactive approach to learning and community engagement, landlords can navigate the complexities of the buy-to-let landscape with greater confidence and success.

# Chapter 5: The Application Process

## Preparing Your Finances

Preparing your finances is a critical step in the buy-to-let process, as it lays the groundwork for a successful investment. Before diving into property purchases, it is essential to assess your current financial situation. This involves reviewing your income, savings, and any existing debts. A clear understanding of your financial health will help you determine how much you can afford to invest in property and what type of mortgage you may qualify for. Calculating your net income and expenses will also provide insight into your cash flow, which is vital for covering ongoing costs associated with being a landlord.

Next, it is important to establish a budget tailored to your buy-to-let ambitions. This budget should include not only the purchase price of the property but also additional costs such as stamp duty, legal fees, and surveyor costs. Furthermore, consider the ongoing expenses of property management, maintenance, and insurance.

By creating a comprehensive budget, you can avoid unexpected financial burdens and ensure that your investment is sustainable in the long run. It is wise to allocate a portion of your budget for unexpected repairs and vacancies, as these can impact your rental income significantly.

Once you have a firm grasp of your finances and a well-structured budget, the next step is to explore your mortgage options. Buy-to-let mortgages differ from residential mortgages in several key ways, including interest rates, deposit requirements, and eligibility criteria. Typically, lenders require a larger deposit for buy-to-let properties, often around 25% of the property's value. Researching various lenders and their products will enable you to find a mortgage that aligns with your investment strategy. It is also advisable to consult with a mortgage broker who specialises in buy-to-let financing, as they can provide tailored advice and help you navigate the complexities of the mortgage market.

As you prepare your finances, consider the potential rental income from your investment property. Conducting thorough market research will help you estimate achievable rental prices in your chosen area.

This information is crucial for calculating your expected yield and understanding how your investment will perform financially. Ensure that your projected rental income covers your mortgage repayments and other costs while providing a suitable return on investment. Understanding the rental market dynamics will also inform your decision-making process regarding property selection and pricing strategies.

Finally, ensure that your financial preparations include a solid contingency plan. The buy-to-let market can be unpredictable, and having a financial buffer can mitigate risks associated with fluctuating property values or changes in rental demand. Setting aside funds to cover at least three to six months of mortgage payments and expenses will provide peace of mind and stability during challenging periods. Additionally, regularly reviewing your financial plan will allow you to adapt to changing circumstances and maintain a healthy investment portfolio. By taking these steps, you will be well-prepared to embark on your buy-to-let journey with confidence.

### Documentation Required

When entering the buy-to-let market in the UK, understanding the documentation required is crucial for a smooth mortgage application process. Lenders typically require a set of documents that verify your identity, financial status, and the property details. The primary document is proof of identity, which can be fulfilled by providing a valid passport or driving license. Additionally, lenders may request a recent utility bill or bank statement to confirm your address. Ensuring that these documents are current and clearly presented will facilitate a quicker assessment by the mortgage provider.

Financial documentation is equally important in the buy-to-let mortgage process. Borrowers must provide evidence of their income, which may include payslips, tax returns, or profit and loss statements for self-employed individuals. Lenders often seek a minimum level of income, typically around £25,000, to ensure that borrowers can manage their financial obligations. Furthermore, proof of existing rental income can bolster your application, demonstrating your capability to maintain positive cash flow from your investment properties.

In addition to personal financial documents, details about the property itself are essential. Lenders will require a copy of the sales memorandum or purchase agreement, as well as information about the property's valuation. A professional valuation is often necessary, as it helps the lender assess the property's worth and ensures it meets their lending criteria. This valuation may include details such as the property's location, condition, and rental potential, all of which can influence the terms of the mortgage offered.

Furthermore, landlords should prepare documentation regarding their existing properties if they own others. This includes providing details of current rental agreements, tenant information, and any existing mortgages. Lenders will want to evaluate your overall portfolio to understand the level of risk involved in your new buy-to-let investment. Having organised records of your existing properties can enhance your credibility and demonstrate your experience as a landlord.

Lastly, additional documentation may include a credit report, which lenders will review to gauge your financial health. A strong credit score can improve your chances of securing favourable mortgage terms.

It is advisable to review your credit report before applying for a buy-to-let mortgage, ensuring that all information is accurate and addressing any discrepancies. By gathering and organising the necessary documentation ahead of time, prospective landlords can streamline the mortgage application process and position themselves for success in the competitive buy-to-let market.

**Submitting Your Application**

Submitting your application for a buy-to-let mortgage is a crucial step in securing funding for your investment property. The process typically begins with gathering the necessary documentation to support your application. Lenders will require proof of your identity, income, and financial stability. This usually includes recent payslips, bank statements, and tax returns if you are self-employed. Additionally, you should prepare a detailed breakdown of your prospective rental income, as lenders will assess whether this income will cover your mortgage repayments.

Once you have compiled your documents, the next step is to choose a mortgage lender.

It is essential to research various lenders and their specific requirements, as these can vary significantly.

Some may have more flexible criteria, while others might offer better interest rates or terms. Comparing these factors can help you make an informed decision. It is also advisable to consult with a mortgage broker who specialises in buy-to-let mortgages. They can provide insights into the best lenders for your situation and assist in navigating the application process.

When you are ready to submit your application, ensure that all forms are completed accurately and that all required documents are included. Missing information or incorrect details can lead to delays or even rejection. Many lenders provide an online application platform, which can simplify the submission process. However, if you prefer a more individualised touch, you can still submit your application in person or via mail, depending on the lender's policies.

After submission, the lender will conduct a thorough assessment of your application. This process often includes a credit check and a property valuation.

The credit check will evaluate your financial history and ability to repay the mortgage, while the property valuation confirms that the property's worth aligns with the loan amount you are requesting. Be prepared for this stage, as it can take several days to weeks, depending on the lender's workload and the complexity of your application.

Once the lender has completed their assessment, they will issue a mortgage offer if everything meets their criteria. It is essential to carefully review this offer, as it will outline the terms of the mortgage, including interest rates, repayment schedules, and any fees involved. If you are satisfied with the terms, you can proceed with the next steps in the purchasing process. Being meticulous during the application stage will set a solid foundation for your buy-to-let investment journey.

# Chapter 6: Understanding Mortgage Terms

### Fixed vs. Variable Rates

When considering buy-to-let mortgages in the UK, one of the most crucial decisions landlords face is choosing between fixed and variable interest rates. Fixed-rate mortgages offer stability, locking in an interest rate for a set period, typically two, five, or even ten years. This predictability can be particularly appealing for landlords who want to budget their monthly expenses without worrying about fluctuating interest rates. With a fixed rate, landlords can calculate their cash flow with certainty, making it easier to plan for property management costs, maintenance, and other expenses associated with rental properties.

On the other hand, variable-rate mortgages can be more flexible and may initially offer lower interest rates than fixed-rate options. These mortgages often come with a base rate tied to the Bank of England's interest rate, meaning that when the base rate rises, so does the mortgage rate.

For buy-to-let investors who are comfortable with market fluctuations, a variable rate can provide the opportunity to benefit from lower payments during periods of low interest rates. However, this option comes with the risk of rising costs if the economy shifts or inflation increases, potentially impacting the profitability of a rental property.

The choice between fixed and variable rates also involves considering the current economic climate and interest rate trends. In a period of rising interest rates, locking in a fixed rate may protect landlords from future increases, making it a prudent choice for those planning long-term investments. Conversely, in a low-interest environment, a variable rate may offer more immediate savings, especially for landlords who anticipate selling or refinancing within a few years. Understanding the current market conditions can help landlords make a more informed decision that aligns with their investment strategy.

Furthermore, landlords must evaluate their tolerance for risk when selecting between fixed and variable rates.

Fixed-rate mortgages provide peace of mind, particularly for those who may not have a financial buffer to absorb potential increases in monthly payments. In contrast, experienced investors who have a solid understanding of market dynamics may opt for variable rates, leveraging their knowledge to capitalise on lower rates while managing the potential risks of market fluctuations. Each landlord's unique financial situation and investment goals will play a significant role in this decision.

The choice between fixed and variable rates should be based on a thorough assessment of personal circumstances, market conditions, and financial goals. Landlords should consider consulting with mortgage advisors who specialise in buy-to-let properties to navigate the complexities of mortgage products. By weighing the advantages and disadvantages of each option, landlords can select a mortgage strategy that aligns with their investment philosophy and enhances their buy-to-let portfolio's overall performance.

## Repayment vs. Interest-Only Mortgages

Repayment and interest-only mortgages represent two fundamental approaches to funding property investments in the UK's buy-to-let market. Understanding the differences between these mortgage types is crucial for landlords aiming to maximise their returns while managing financial risk.

A repayment mortgage requires the borrower to pay back both the capital and interest over the term of the loan. This structure ensures that, by the end of the mortgage term, the property will be fully owned without any remaining debt. Many landlords opt for this route as it provides a clear path to ownership and can contribute positively to their credit profile.

In contrast, an interest-only mortgage allows the borrower to pay only the interest on the loan for a specified period, with the principal amount remaining unchanged. This approach can be particularly appealing to buy-to-let investors seeking to minimise monthly outgoings and maximise cash flow. However, it comes with the significant obligation of repaying the full principal at the end of the term.

Investors must have a solid withdrawal plan in place, which often involves selling the property or refinancing to ensure they can settle the outstanding balance when due.

Cash flow management is a critical consideration for landlords when choosing between these mortgage types. With repayment mortgages, monthly payments are higher due to the inclusion of capital repayments, which can strain cash flow, especially in the early years of ownership. However, as the mortgage balance decreases, landlords may find their equity in the property increases, providing a buffer against market fluctuations. On the other hand, interest-only mortgages allow for lower initial payments, enabling landlords to reinvest the savings into property improvements or additional acquisitions, potentially accelerating growth in their portfolios.

Another crucial factor is the risk associated with each mortgage type. With repayment mortgages, the risk is relatively low as landlords gradually build equity, and the obligation to repay reduces over time. Conversely, interest-only mortgages can pose risks if property values decline, or rental income fluctuates.

If a landlord is unable to repay the principal at the end of the mortgage term, they may face financial challenges. Therefore, thorough market research and financial planning are essential for anyone considering this option in the buy-to-let sector.

Ultimately, the choice between repayment and interest-only mortgages will depend on individual financial circumstances, investment strategy, and risk tolerance. Landlords should carefully evaluate their short-term cash flow needs against long-term investment goals. Consulting with mortgage advisors can provide valuable insights tailored to specific situations, ensuring that the chosen mortgage aligns with the overall investment strategy and financial objectives in the competitive buy-to-let market.

### Fees and Charges

When considering buy to let mortgages, understanding the fees and charges involved is essential for landlords to make informed financial decisions. These costs can significantly impact profitability, and they extend beyond the basic mortgage repayments.

Typical fees associated with buy to let mortgages include arrangement fees, valuation fees, and legal fees. Arrangement fees, which can range from a few hundred to several thousand pounds, are charged by lenders for setting up the mortgage. It is crucial for landlords to compare these fees across different lenders, as they can vary widely and affect the overall cost of borrowing.

Valuation fees are another important consideration, as lenders require a property valuation before approving a mortgage. This fee typically ranges from £150 to £1,500, depending on the property's value and location. A professional valuation ensures that the lender is protected against over-lending, but landlords should account for this cost in their budget. Additionally, some lenders may offer free valuations as part of promotional deals, which can be an attractive option for cost-conscious investors. Understanding these fees allows landlords to anticipate their upfront costs and avoid unpleasant surprises.

Legal fees are also a significant expense when securing a buy to let mortgage. Landlords will need to hire a solicitor or conveyancer to manage the legal aspects of property purchase.

These fees can vary based on the complexity of the transaction and the solicitor's experience, typically ranging from £500 to £1,500. It is advisable for landlords to obtain quotes from multiple legal professionals and clarify what services are included in the fee. This ensures that they receive the best value for their money while ensuring all legal requirements are met.

In addition to these one-time fees, landlords should also consider ongoing charges, such as management fees if they choose to hire a letting agent. These fees can be a percentage of the rental income, typically between 8% and 15%, depending on the services provided. Using a letting agent can save time and effort, but landlords must weigh these costs against the benefits of self-managing their properties. Additionally, landlords should be aware of potential maintenance costs, insurance premiums, and service charges, which can add to the overall expenditure associated with buy to let investments.

Finally, it is essential for landlords to factor in the possibility of early repayment charges if they decide to pay off their mortgage early or switch to a better deal.

Many lenders impose penalties for early repayment, which can deter landlords from making changes to their mortgage arrangements. Understanding these fees and charges upfront enables landlords to create a comprehensive financial plan, ensuring that their buy to let venture remains profitable in the long term. By being well-informed about all aspects of fees and charges, landlords can navigate the buy to let landscape more effectively and make decisions that align with their investment goals.

# Chapter 7: Choosing the Right Lender

## Comparing Mortgage Products

When navigating the buy-to-let landscape, understanding the various mortgage products available is crucial for landlords seeking to maximise their investments. Buy-to-let mortgages differ significantly from standard residential mortgages, primarily in their purpose and eligibility criteria. These specialised loans are tailored for individuals purchasing property with the intent of renting it out. Therefore, lenders assess the potential rental income alongside the borrower's financial situation, making it essential for landlords to familiarise themselves with the distinct characteristics of each mortgage product.

Fixed-rate mortgages are one of the most common options for buy-to-let investors. This type of mortgage offers a consistent interest rate over a specified period, usually ranging from two to ten years. The predictability of fixed monthly payments can be advantageous for landlords, as it allows for better budgeting and financial planning.

However, while fixed-rate mortgages provide stability, they may come with higher initial interest rates compared to variable rate options. Landlords must weigh the benefits of consistent payments against potential savings offered by variable rates, especially in a fluctuating market.

Variable-rate mortgages present an alternative that can be appealing in a low-interest environment. These mortgages typically have interest rates that can change over time, based on the lender's base rate. While this could lead to lower initial payments, it also introduces uncertainty, as payments may increase if interest rates rise. Landlords who opt for variable-rate mortgages should be prepared for the possibility of fluctuating costs and consider whether they can absorb potential increases in their monthly outgoings. This option may be more suitable for experienced investors comfortable with some level of risk.

Another product to consider is the interest-only mortgage, which allows landlords to pay only the interest on the loan for a specified period, rather than the principal.

This arrangement can create lower initial monthly payments, freeing up cash flow for other investments or expenses. However, landlords need a solid repayment strategy for the principal, as the full loan amount will be due at the end of the mortgage term. This type of mortgage can be attractive to those who are confident in their ability to sell the property for a profit or refinance before the repayment period arrives.

Finally, landlords should also explore limited company buy-to-let mortgages, which are designed for those purchasing properties through a corporate entity. This product may offer tax advantages, particularly in the wake of changes to tax relief on mortgage interest. Limited company mortgages typically have different lending criteria and may feature slightly higher interest rates than personal buy-to-let mortgages. Investors must evaluate whether the benefits of incorporating outweigh the costs and complexities involved in operating as a limited company. By comparing these various mortgage products, landlords can make informed decisions that align with their investment strategies and financial goals.

## Understanding Lender Criteria

Understanding the criteria that lenders use to assess buy-to-let mortgage applications is essential for landlords looking to expand their portfolios. Lenders typically evaluate several key factors, including the borrower's credit history, rental income potential, and the overall property value. Each lender may have specific requirements, but there are commonalities that can help prospective landlords prepare their applications more effectively.

Credit history plays a pivotal role in the lender's decision-making process. A strong credit score demonstrates financial responsibility and an ability to manage debt, which can lead to better mortgage terms and interest rates. Landlords should be aware of their credit reports, ensuring that there are no inaccuracies or outstanding debts that could negatively impact their scores. It is advisable to address any credit issues before applying for a mortgage, as this can enhance the chances of approval and favourable terms.

Another critical factor is the rental income potential of the property.

Lenders typically require a thorough assessment of the anticipated rental income to ensure that it meets a minimum threshold, often set at 125% to 145% of the mortgage payment. This is known as the "rental cover ratio." Landlords should prepare to provide evidence of rental demand in the area, such as recent rental listings, average rental prices, and occupancy rates.

Understanding local market conditions can significantly strengthen a mortgage application.

The property's value and condition also weigh heavily in the lender's evaluation. Lenders need to ensure that the property is suitable for rental purposes and has the potential to generate consistent income. A property valuation will be conducted to assess its market value, and any necessary repairs or issues that could affect its rental prospects may need to be addressed beforehand. Landlords should consider obtaining a professional valuation or appraisal to better understand how their property is perceived in the market.

Finally, different lenders may have varying criteria based on their risk appetite and target market. Some may focus on the experience of the landlord, while others may prioritise the property's location or type. It is crucial for landlords to shop around and compare different lenders' criteria, as this can lead to more favourable borrowing options. Understanding these nuances will empower landlords to make informed decisions when selecting a mortgage provider, supporting their investment strategies in the buy-to-let market.

**The Role of Mortgage Brokers**

Mortgage brokers play a crucial role in the buy-to-let market, acting as intermediaries between landlords and lenders. They possess extensive knowledge of the mortgage landscape, which can be particularly beneficial for landlords looking to navigate the complexities of buy-to-let mortgages. With various lenders offering different products and terms, a mortgage broker can help landlords identify the most suitable mortgage options tailored to their investment strategies and financial situations.

One of the significant advantages of working with a mortgage broker is their access to a wide range of mortgage products. Unlike individual borrowers who may only have visibility into a handful of lenders, brokers have established relationships with numerous financial institutions.

This access allows them to present landlords with a variety of choices, including competitive interest rates and flexible lending criteria. Additionally, brokers often have insights into exclusive deals that are not advertised directly to the public, enabling landlords to secure better financing terms.

Mortgage brokers also provide invaluable assistance in the application process. The paperwork involved in securing a mortgage can be overwhelming, especially for first-time landlords. Brokers are adept at managing the documentation required, ensuring that everything is submitted accurately and on time. They also help landlords prepare for potential challenges during the underwriting process, such as questions regarding the property's rental potential or the landlord's creditworthiness. This proactive support can significantly streamline the process and reduce the time it takes to secure financing.

Furthermore, brokers offer personalised advice based on the specific needs and goals of the landlord. They take the time to understand the landlord's investment plans, whether they are looking to purchase a single property or expand a portfolio. This tailored approach allows brokers to recommend mortgage products that align with the landlord's cash flow expectations and long-term objectives. By considering factors such as rental income, property appreciation, and tax implications, brokers can guide landlords toward making informed decisions that enhance their investment potential.

Finally, the expertise of mortgage brokers can prove invaluable in a rapidly changing financial landscape. As the economy fluctuates and regulatory environments evolve, brokers stay updated on industry trends and changes that may impact buy-to-let financing. This ongoing education allows them to provide landlords with timely advice and strategic insights, ensuring that their financing decisions remain aligned with market conditions. By leveraging the knowledge and support of a mortgage broker, landlords can navigate the complexities of buy-to-let mortgages with confidence.

# Chapter 8: Managing Your Buy to Let Property

**Tenant Selection**

Tenant selection is a critical aspect of property management that can influence the success of your buy-to-let investment. A well-chosen tenant can ensure timely rent payments, maintain the property in good condition, and contribute positively to the community. Conversely, a poor selection can lead to financial loss, property damage, and a prolonged eviction process. Therefore, landlords must adopt a systematic approach to tenant selection, balancing thoroughness with efficiency to find the right fit for their properties.

The first step in tenant selection involves advertising the property effectively. Landlords should highlight the key features and benefits of the property, such as its location, amenities, and any recent renovations. Using multiple platforms, including online property portals, social media, and local advertising, can increase visibility and attract a diverse range of potential tenants.

Clear and appealing photographs, alongside an accurate and detailed description, will help to draw in serious inquiries and set the stage for a successful tenant search.

Once applications start coming in, landlords must implement a stringent screening process. This typically includes background checks, credit checks, and references from previous landlords. A credit check provides insight into the applicant's financial history, while references can confirm their reliability as a tenant. It is also prudent to verify employment status and income level to ensure that the prospective tenant can afford the rent. By gathering this information, landlords can make informed decisions and reduce the risk of future issues.

Another critical factor in tenant selection is understanding the legal obligations surrounding discrimination. Landlords must adhere to the Equality Act 2010, which prohibits discrimination based on protected characteristics such as race, gender, age, and disability. It is essential to approach tenant selection fairly and impartially, ensuring that all applicants are treated equally and without bias.

This not only helps to avoid legal repercussions but also fosters a positive reputation within the community, which can be beneficial for future rental opportunities.

Finally, it is important for landlords to trust their instincts and consider the overall demeanour and attitude of prospective tenants during viewings and interviews. While financial checks are vital, a tenant's attitude can often give insights into their potential behaviour as a renter. Engaging in open and honest conversations can help landlords gauge whether an applicant is likely to respect the property and maintain a positive relationship. By combining thorough screening with a personal touch, landlords can enhance their chances of selecting reliable tenants who will contribute positively to their buy-to-let investment.

**Property Management Options**

Property management is a critical component of the buy-to-let sector, influencing both the efficiency of operations and the overall profitability of rental investments. Landlords have several management options available, each with distinct advantages and disadvantages.

Understanding these choices can help landlords make informed decisions that align with their investment goals and personal circumstances.

One popular option is self-management, where landlords take on the responsibility of managing their properties directly. This approach can save on management fees, allowing landlords to maximise their rental income. Self-managing landlords handle all aspects of property management, including tenant sourcing, rent collection, maintenance, and compliance with legal obligations. While this option offers control and flexibility, it also demands significant time and effort, as well as a solid understanding of tenancy laws and market conditions.

Alternatively, landlords can choose to collaborate with a letting agent. This option provides a more hands-off approach to property management, allowing landlords to delegate responsibilities to professionals. Letting agents typically offer a range of services, from tenant finding to full property management. This can be particularly beneficial for landlords who may not have the time or expertise to effectively manage their properties.

However, this convenience comes at a cost, as agents usually charge a percentage of the rental income or a flat fee for their services, which can impact overall profitability.

Another option to consider is hybrid property management, which combines elements of both self-management and professional services. In this model, landlords may choose to handle specific tasks themselves while outsourcing others to a letting agent. For example, a landlord might manage tenant communications and maintenance issues but rely on an agent for rent collection and legal compliance. This approach allows landlords to maintain a level of control while still benefiting from the expertise of professionals in areas where they may lack knowledge or resources.

Finally, property management software has emerged as a modern solution for landlords looking to streamline their operations. These platforms can help landlords manage tenants, track rental payments, and maintain property records efficiently. By utilising technology, landlords can automate many aspects of property management, reducing the administrative burden and allowing them to focus on their investment strategy.

While not a substitute for professional management or self-management, property management software can enhance efficiency and help landlords make data-driven decisions. Each of these property management options has its unique features, and landlords should carefully evaluate their own needs, resources, and investment goals to choose the most suitable approach.

**Legal Responsibilities and Compliance**

In the realm of buy-to-let investments, understanding legal responsibilities and compliance is paramount for landlords. The UK property market is governed by a complex framework of laws and regulations that dictate how landlords must operate. These regulations encompass various aspects, including tenant rights, property standards, and health and safety requirements. Failing to adhere to these laws not only jeopardises the investment but can also lead to legal repercussions, including fines and potential loss of rental income.

One of the key legal responsibilities for landlords is the obligation to ensure that the property is safe and compliant with health and safety regulations.

This includes conducting regular gas safety checks, ensuring electrical installations are safe, and maintaining adequate fire safety measures. Landlords must provide evidence of compliance, such as gas safety certificates and electrical safety reports, which must be updated regularly. Failure to meet these safety standards not only places tenants at risk but can also expose landlords to significant liabilities.

Another critical area of compliance relates to tenant rights and protections. The Tenant Fees Act 2019 introduced significant changes to the fees landlords can charge and established a framework for transparency in rental agreements. Landlords are required to provide tenants with a written tenancy agreement that outlines their rights and responsibilities, as well as those of the landlord. Additionally, landlords must ensure that deposits are protected in a government-approved tenancy deposit scheme, further safeguarding tenants' interests and promoting fair practices in the rental market.

Landlords must also be mindful of anti-discrimination laws and ensure compliance with the Equality Act 2010.

This legislation prohibits discrimination against tenants based on characteristics such as race, gender, disability, and age. It is essential for landlords to foster an inclusive environment and ensure that their rental practices do not unfairly disadvantage any group. Regular training and awareness of these laws can help landlords avoid unintentional discrimination and create a fair rental process.

Finally, staying informed about changes in legislation is crucial for compliance and successful property management. The UK housing market is subject to ongoing reforms, and landlords must keep abreast of new laws and amendments that may affect their operations. This may involve joining landlord associations, attending workshops, or consulting with legal professionals. By prioritising legal responsibilities and compliance, landlords can protect their investments, provide safe and secure homes for tenants, and contribute positively to the rental market.

# Chapter 9: Tax Implications for Landlords

## Income Tax on Rental Income

Rental income is a significant aspect of the buy-to-let investment landscape, and understanding the tax implications is crucial for landlords in the UK. When a property is rented out, the income generated is subject to income tax, and this can affect the overall profitability of the investment. Landlords must report their rental income on their self-assessment tax return, and it is vital to accurately calculate the amount owed to avoid penalties and potential audits by HM Revenue and Customs (HMRC).

Landlords can deduct certain allowable expenses from their rental income before calculating their taxable profit. These expenses may include mortgage interest, letting agent fees, maintenance and repairs, and insurance costs. It is important to differentiate between allowable and non-allowable expenses, as only the former can be subtracted from gross rental income to arrive at the taxable figure.

Careful record-keeping of all expenses throughout the year will facilitate this process and ensure that landlords maximise their deductions.

The taxation of rental income in the UK operates on a progressive tax rate system, meaning that the overall tax owed will depend on the landlord's total income, including rental income and any other earnings. Landlords may fall into different tax brackets based on their combined income, which can range from the basic rate to the higher or additional rate. Understanding where one's income falls within these brackets is essential for effective financial planning and for anticipating tax liabilities.

In recent years, changes in tax legislation have specifically impacted buy-to-let landlords. Most notably, the phasing out of mortgage interest relief has altered the way landlords can claim tax relief on their finance costs. Instead of being able to deduct these costs from their rental income, landlords now receive a tax credit based on 20% of their mortgage interest payments.

This reform can significantly affect higher-rate taxpayers, potentially elevating their overall tax burden and influencing investment strategies moving forward.

Lastly, landlords should consider the implications of capital gains tax when selling a rental property. While this tax is not related to rental income, it is a critical component of overall tax planning for property investors. When a property is sold at a profit, the capital gain is subject to tax, which can be substantial depending on the length of ownership and the increase in property value. Understanding the full scope of taxation on rental income and property sales will empower landlords to make more informed decisions regarding their buy-to-let investments and ensure compliance with UK tax laws.

**Capital Gains Tax**

Capital gains tax (CGT) is a crucial consideration for landlords and property investors in the UK, particularly those engaged in buy to let ventures. When a property is sold for more than its original purchase price, the profit made is subject to CGT.

Understanding how this tax works is essential for effective financial planning and can significantly impact the overall return on investment. The current tax rate for individuals varies depending on their income tax bracket, with basic rate taxpayers paying 18% on residential property gains and higher or additional rate taxpayers facing a 24% charge.

It is important for landlords to be aware of the allowances available that can reduce their CGT liability. The most notable is the annual exempt amount, which allows individuals to make a certain level of profit each year without incurring tax. For the tax year 2024/25, this exemption is £3,000. Additionally, if a property has been a primary residence at any point, landlords may qualify for private residence relief, which can further mitigate the taxable gain. Understanding these exemptions is vital for landlords seeking to maximise their profits while minimising tax obligations.

When calculating the capital gains, landlords should also consider the allowable costs that can be deducted from the sale price. These costs include expenses incurred during the purchase, such as legal fees, stamp duty, and various improvements made to the property.

It is essential to maintain accurate records of these expenses, as they can significantly reduce the taxable gain. Furthermore, any costs directly associated with the sale, like estate agent fees, can also be factored into the calculation, leading to a lower CGT bill.

For landlords who may be considering transferring property ownership or gifting properties to family members, it is crucial to understand the implications of CGT in these situations. Transferring property can trigger a CGT liability, as the market value at the time of transfer is considered. However, there are specific reliefs available, such as gifts to spouses or civil partners, which are typically exempt from CGT. Being informed about these rules can help landlords make strategic decisions about property ownership and succession planning.

Finally, it is worth noting that the rules surrounding capital gains tax can be complex and subject to change. Therefore, it is advisable for landlords to consult with a financial advisor or tax professional to ensure compliance and to optimise their tax strategy.

This professional guidance can provide peace of mind and ensure that landlords are well-prepared for any potential tax liabilities that arise from their buy to let activities, contributing to a more successful investment experience.

**Tax Reliefs and Allowances**

Tax reliefs and allowances play a crucial role in enhancing the profitability of buy-to-let investments in the UK. Understanding these financial tools can significantly impact a landlord's overall return on investment. The UK tax system offers various reliefs designed to help landlords manage their tax liabilities more effectively. By being aware of these provisions, landlords can make informed decisions that maximise their investment returns.

One of the primary tax reliefs available to landlords is the ability to deduct allowable expenses from their rental income. These expenses can include mortgage interest, letting agent fees, maintenance costs, and utilities paid by the landlord. Since these expenses reduce the taxable rental income, landlords effectively lower their overall tax burden.

It is essential for landlords to keep accurate records of all expenses, as this documentation will be required when filing tax returns and can substantiate claims made to HM Revenue and Customs (HMRC).

Another significant allowance for landlords is the Wear and Tear Allowance, which was available until April 2016. Although it has been replaced by a new system that allows landlords to deduct the actual cost of replacing furnishings and fittings, understanding the transition is important. Landlords can now claim tax relief on the actual costs incurred, which can lead to substantial savings, particularly if they frequently upgrade or replace items in their properties. This change encourages landlords to invest in higher-quality furnishings, potentially improving tenant satisfaction and retention rates.

Capital Gains Tax (CGT) is another critical consideration for landlords, especially when selling a property. When a buy-to-let property is sold, the profit made above the purchase price may be subject to CGT.

However, landlords can benefit from certain reliefs, such as Private Residence Relief and Letting Relief, which can mitigate tax liabilities if the property was once their main residence.

Understanding these reliefs and planning the timing of a sale can significantly impact the amount of CGT owed, making it crucial for landlords to seek professional advice when considering property sales.

Finally, tax reliefs specific to buy-to-let mortgages also play a vital role in a landlord's financial strategy. Interest payments on buy-to-let mortgages can be deducted from rental income, reducing the overall taxable income. However, changes introduced in recent years have restricted the tax relief available on mortgage interest, transitioning to a system where landlords receive a tax credit based on a percentage of their mortgage interest payments. Navigating these changes requires careful planning and an understanding of how they affect overall profitability, making it essential for landlords to stay informed about current tax laws and seek guidance where necessary.

# Chapter 10: Refinancing Your Buy to Let Mortgage

## When and Why to Refinance

Refinancing a buy-to-let mortgage can be a strategic move for landlords looking to improve their financial position. Understanding when to refinance hinges on several factors, including interest rates, property value, and personal financial goals. A common reason for refinancing is to take advantage of lower interest rates. If the market has shifted since your original mortgage agreement, a lower rate could significantly reduce your monthly payments, increasing cash flow and enhancing profitability. Evaluating the current rate environment and comparing it against your existing mortgage can reveal potential savings that warrant the refinance process.

Another critical factor influencing the decision to refinance is the increase in property value. If your rental property has appreciated since the initial purchase, you may be able to refinance to access the increased equity.

This equity can be used for various purposes, including funding further property investments, making improvements to the existing property, or consolidating debt. By tapping into this equity, landlords can leverage their assets to grow their portfolios and improve their overall financial standing while potentially enhancing the property's rental income.

The terms of your current mortgage also play a significant role in the refinancing decision. If your existing mortgage has unfavourable terms, such as a high-interest rate or limited flexibility, refinancing may be beneficial. Additionally, if you find that your financial situation has improved and you qualify for better mortgage terms, this can lead to more favourable repayment conditions. A lower interest rate or a switch from an interest-only to a repayment mortgage could enhance your financial strategy, allowing you to build equity in the property more effectively over time.

Timing is crucial in the refinancing process. Market conditions, personal circumstances, and the overall economic environment can all impact the optimal moment to refinance. Landlords should monitor interest rate trends and be aware of any economic forecasts that could influence borrowing costs.

Furthermore, personal financial stability, such as employment status and credit score, can affect refinancing eligibility and terms. It is advisable to conduct a thorough assessment of both market conditions and personal finances before deciding to refinance.

In conclusion, refinancing can be a valuable tool for landlords in the buy-to-let market, but it requires careful consideration of multiple factors. Evaluating the timing, interest rates, property values, and personal financial goals will help landlords determine whether refinancing is a suitable option. By making informed decisions, landlords can optimise their mortgage arrangements, improve cash flow, and enhance the profitability of their rental properties.

**The Refinancing Process**

The refinancing process involves assessing your current mortgage situation and determining whether it makes financial sense to switch to a new lender or product. For buy-to-let landlords, this is particularly relevant as market conditions and interest rates fluctuate. The first step in the refinancing journey is to evaluate your existing mortgage terms and the overall performance of your rental property.

This includes reviewing the interest rate, fees, and any penalties for early repayment. Understanding these elements will help you gauge the potential benefits of refinancing and whether it aligns with your investment strategy.

Once you have a clear picture of your current mortgage, the next step is to research potential lenders and mortgage products. The UK buy-to-let market offers a variety of options, from fixed-rate mortgages to tracker deals, each with its own set of advantages and disadvantages. It is crucial to compare these products based on factors such as interest rates, fees, and terms. Additionally, considering the lender's criteria for buy-to-let mortgages is essential, as they often require specific documentation, including proof of rental income and property valuation reports. This research phase is vital to ensure that you are making a well-informed decision.

After narrowing down your options, the next phase is to gather the necessary documentation for the refinancing application. This typically includes income statements, tax returns, and property information.

Some lenders may also request additional details, such as the rental agreements and a comprehensive overview of your financial circumstances.

Being organised and prepared can streamline the process, allowing for quicker approvals and less hassle. It is advisable to maintain clear communication with your chosen lender to understand the specific requirements and to ensure that your application stands out.

Upon application submission, the lender will conduct a thorough assessment of your financial situation and the property's value. This process often includes an appraisal of the property to confirm its market value, which influences the amount they are willing to lend. The lender will also evaluate your creditworthiness, considering your credit history and current financial obligations. Understanding that this stage can take time is essential, as lenders may have different processing times. Patience and responsiveness to any requests for additional information will facilitate a smoother refinancing experience.

Once your application has been approved, you will receive a formal offer outlining the new mortgage terms. It is crucial to review this offer carefully, comparing it to your existing mortgage to ensure that the new terms provide a tangible financial benefit. If you decide to proceed, the final step is to complete the legal paperwork and finalise the refinancing process. This may involve additional costs, such as legal fees and valuation fees, which should be factored into your overall cost-benefit analysis. Successfully navigating the refinancing process can enhance your investment portfolio, improve cash flow, and potentially increase your property's equity.

**Potential Pitfalls**

When entering the buy-to-let market, landlords must be aware of several potential pitfalls that can significantly impact their investment. One of the most common issues is underestimating the costs associated with property management. Many new landlords focus solely on the mortgage payments, neglecting other expenses such as maintenance, insurance, property management fees, and unexpected repairs.

These costs can quickly accumulate and erode profit margins, especially if the property requires extensive work or if tenants cause damage.

Another potential pitfall is the impact of changing regulations and legislation affecting the rental market. The UK government frequently updates laws pertaining to tenancy agreements, safety regulations, and tax implications. Landlords who fail to keep abreast of these changes risk non-compliance, which can lead to fines or legal disputes. Staying informed and investing in professional advice is essential to navigate this dynamic landscape successfully.

Tenant selection is another critical area where landlords can encounter difficulties. Choosing the wrong tenant can have severe financial implications, including late or missed rent payments and property damage. Conducting thorough background checks, including credit history and previous landlord references, is vital. However, some landlords may rush this process or allow personal biases to influence their decisions, resulting in problematic tenancies that could be avoided with due diligence.

Market fluctuations present an inherent risk in the buy-to-let sector. Property values can rise and fall due to various factors, including economic conditions, interest rates, and local demand. Landlords who fail to consider these fluctuations may overestimate their property's value or struggle to sell or re-finance if necessary. Understanding the local market trends and conducting regular property valuations can help mitigate this risk and ensure informed decision-making.

Finally, one of the most significant pitfalls landlords face is inadequate financial planning. Many new landlords enter the market without a clear financial strategy, relying solely on rental income to cover expenses. This approach can backfire if there are extended periods without tenants or if unexpected expenses arise. Establishing a financial buffer, alongside a strategic plan for growth and reinvestment, can provide the security needed to weather market uncertainties and maintain profitability in the long run.

## Chapter 11: Future Trends in Buy to Let

### Emerging Markets

Emerging markets present a unique opportunity for buy-to-let investors looking to diversify their portfolios and maximise returns. In the context of the UK real estate sector, these markets often refer to areas experiencing rapid economic growth, urbanisation, and rising demand for rental properties. Investors can capitalise on these trends by identifying neighbourhoods that are undergoing regeneration or development, which can lead to increased property values and rental yields. Understanding local economic indicators and demographic shifts is crucial for spotting these emerging markets.

One key factor to consider when evaluating emerging markets is infrastructure development. Areas benefiting from new transport links, schools, and commercial projects are typically more attractive to potential tenants. For instance, cities that are expanding their public transport networks may experience an influx of residents who prefer to live near these amenities.

As an investor, it is essential to analyse planned infrastructure projects and their projected impact on property demand. Keeping an eye on local government initiatives and funding allocations can provide valuable insights into which areas are likely to flourish.

Another important aspect of emerging markets is the demographic profile of the area. Young professionals and families seeking affordable housing often gravitate towards up-and-coming neighbourhoods. Investors should research population growth rates, employment opportunities, and lifestyle amenities to gauge the attractiveness of a location. Areas with a strong presence of universities or major employers can be particularly appealing for buy-to-let investments, as they typically ensure a steady stream of potential tenants. Understanding the needs and preferences of the target demographic can help landlords make informed decisions about property types and rental strategies.

It is also vital to assess the regulatory environment when considering emerging markets for buy-to-let investments.

Local laws regarding rental properties, tenant rights, and property management can vary significantly from one area to another. Investors should conduct thorough due diligence to ensure compliance with local regulations and to understand any potential risks involved. Engaging with local real estate experts, property management companies, and legal advisors can provide insights into navigating the complexities of the market.

Finally, while emerging markets offer significant potential for growth, they also come with inherent risks. Property values in these areas can be volatile, and the success of an investment may depend on broader economic conditions. Investors must maintain a balanced approach by conducting comprehensive market research, keeping abreast of economic trends, and considering the long-term viability of their investments. By understanding the dynamics of emerging markets and employing strategic planning, buy-to-let investors can enhance their chances of success in a competitive landscape.

## Changes in Legislation

Changes in legislation have significant implications for landlords operating in the buy-to-let market in the UK.

These legislative shifts are often introduced to adapt to economic conditions, address housing shortages, or respond to social issues such as tenant rights and housing standards. Understanding these changes is crucial for landlords to navigate the complexities of property investment effectively.

Staying informed about the evolving legal landscape can help mitigate risks and enhance the profitability of buy-to-let ventures. One notable change in legislation is the introduction of stricter safety regulations for rental properties.

Landlords are now required to ensure that their properties meet specific safety standards, including electrical safety checks and gas safety certifications.

Failure to comply can lead to significant penalties, including fines and potential criminal charges.

These regulations aim to protect tenants and ensure that rental properties are safe and habitable, thereby increasing the responsibility of landlords to maintain their properties.

Another critical area of legislative change is the evolving landscape of tenant rights. Recent laws have enhanced protections for tenants, including regulations against unfair evictions and the requirement for landlords to provide a minimum notice period before terminating a tenancy.

This shift aims to create a more balanced relationship between landlords and tenants, allowing for greater stability in the rental market. For landlords, this means adapting their business practices to comply with these regulations while also promoting positive relationships with their tenants.

Taxation is also a pivotal aspect of legislation that has undergone significant changes in recent years. The reduction of mortgage interest tax relief has impacted many landlords, leading to increased costs and lower profitability. Additionally, changes to Capital Gains Tax rules have implications for landlords considering the sale of their properties.

It is essential for landlords to consult with tax professionals to understand how these changes affect their financial strategies and to explore potential tax relief options available to them.

Moreover, the introduction of new regulations surrounding energy efficiency has prompted landlords to invest in improvements to their properties. The Minimum Energy Efficiency Standards (MEES) require rental properties to achieve a certain Energy Performance Certificate (EPC) rating. This legislation is designed to encourage sustainable practices in the rental market and improve the overall quality of housing stock. For landlords, this means not only complying with the law but also potentially increasing property value and appeal to environmentally conscious tenants.

In summary, changes in legislation surrounding buy-to-let properties in the UK require landlords to remain vigilant and proactive. Adapting to new safety regulations, understanding enhanced tenant rights, navigating tax implications, and complying with energy efficiency standards are all essential components of successful property management.

By staying informed and responsive to these legislative changes, landlords can better protect their investments while contributing positively to the rental market.

## Adapting to Market Changes

Adapting to market changes is crucial for landlords operating within the buy-to-let sector in the UK. The real estate market is inherently dynamic, influenced by economic fluctuations, changes in government policy, and evolving tenant preferences.

Landlords must be proactive in understanding these shifts to maintain profitability and ensure their investments remain viable. This involves not only monitoring market trends but also being willing to adjust strategies and operations in response to new challenges and opportunities.

One of the key factors affecting the buy-to-let market is interest rates. The Bank of England's decisions on monetary policy can significantly impact mortgage rates, which in turn influence landlords' borrowing costs. When interest rates rise, landlords may face higher mortgage repayments, potentially squeezing their cash flow.

Conversely, a drop in rates can provide an opportunity to refinance existing mortgages at more favourable terms.

Staying informed about interest rate trends enables landlords to make strategic decisions, such as whether to lock in a fixed-rate mortgage or explore variable options.

Government policies, such as tax changes and housing regulations, also play a significant role in shaping the buy-to-let landscape.

Recent years have seen significant reforms, including the phased reduction of mortgage interest tax relief and the introduction of an additional 3% stamp duty for buy-to-let purchases. Understanding these changes is essential for landlords to assess their financial implications and adjust their investment strategies accordingly.

Engaging with professional advisors and industry bodies can provide valuable insights into navigating these regulations effectively.

Tenant preferences have evolved, particularly in response to social and economic trends.

The increasing demand for flexibility, remote work options, and eco-friendly living spaces means landlords must adapt their properties to meet these expectations.

This might involve investing in modern amenities, energy-efficient upgrades, or offering short-term rental options. By keeping a pulse on tenant needs and preferences, landlords can enhance their property's appeal, reduce vacancy rates, and ultimately achieve better rental yields.

Finally, leveraging technology can be a critical element in adapting to market changes. Property management software, online tenant screening tools, and digital marketing strategies can streamline operations and improve tenant engagement. Utilising data analytics can provide insights into market conditions, helping landlords make informed investment decisions. By embracing technological advancements, landlords can not only enhance their operational efficiency but also position themselves competitively in an ever-changing market. Adapting to these shifts is not merely a reactive measure; it is a proactive strategy that can lead to sustained success in the buy-to-let arena.

# Chapter 12: Conclusion

## Summarising Key Points

In the realm of buy to let investments, understanding the key points surrounding mortgages is crucial for landlords aiming to optimise their portfolios. Primarily, it is essential to recognise the different types of buy to let mortgages available in the UK. These typically include fixed-rate mortgages, where the interest rate remains constant for a specified period, and variable-rate mortgages, which can fluctuate based on market conditions. Each type carries its own advantages and disadvantages, making it important for landlords to assess their financial situations and investment strategies before selecting the most suitable option.

Another critical aspect to consider is the deposit requirements. Most lenders in the UK require a minimum deposit of 25% of the property's value for buy to let mortgages. However, this figure can vary based on the lender, the property type, and the landlord's financial history. A larger deposit can often lead to more favourable mortgage terms and lower interest rates, enhancing the investment's profitability.

Landlords should also be aware of deposit sources, as lenders may scrutinise the origin of these funds to ensure compliance with regulations.

Furthermore, understanding the importance of rental income is vital for securing a buy to let mortgage. Lenders typically assess the potential rental yield of the property to ensure it meets their criteria for affordability. They look for rental income to cover at least 125% of the mortgage payments, factoring in an interest rate buffer.

This means that landlords should conduct thorough market research to determine realistic rental prices in their target areas, as this will significantly influence their mortgage approval chances and overall investment viability.

In addition to the financial aspects, landlords must also familiarise themselves with the legal requirements associated with buy to let properties. This includes being aware of regulations surrounding tenant rights, property safety standards, and licensing obligations, which can vary by locality.

Compliance with these laws not only protects landlords from potential legal issues but also enhances their reputation as responsible property owners, attracting quality tenants and ensuring smoother rental operations.

Finally, regular reviews of mortgage agreements and staying informed about market trends can make a significant difference in a landlord's investment strategy. The buy to let landscape is continually evolving, influenced by changes in interest rates, government policies, and economic conditions. By periodically reassessing their mortgage terms and exploring opportunities for remortgaging, landlords can capitalise on better rates or more favourable conditions, maximising their returns and ensuring the long-term success of their investment ventures.

## Final Thoughts on Buy to Let Mortgages

As the landscape of property investment continues to evolve, buy to let mortgages remain a critical tool for landlords in the UK. Understanding the intricacies of these financial products is essential for anyone looking to maximise their property investment. The stability of buy to let mortgages allows landlords to leverage their investments while providing the opportunity for capital growth and rental income. However, it is crucial to approach these mortgages with a clear understanding of the risks and responsibilities that come with them.

One of the key considerations for prospective buy to let investors is the importance of thorough financial planning. Before committing to a mortgage, investors should assess their financial situation, including their ability to cover mortgage payments during void periods when the property may not be generating rental income. Additionally, factors such as interest rates, property management costs, and potential maintenance issues should be factored into the overall budget. A well-thought-out financial plan can help mitigate risks and enhance the potential for a successful investment.

Moreover, understanding the different types of buy to let mortgages available is vital for making informed decisions. Fixed-rate mortgages offer stability in monthly repayments, while variable-rate options may provide flexibility but come with the risk of fluctuating costs. Investors should evaluate their long-term plans and risk tolerance when selecting a mortgage type. Consulting with a mortgage advisor who specialises in buy to let can provide valuable insights into finding the most suitable product for individual circumstances.

Regulatory changes and tax implications also play a significant role in the buy to let market. Investors must stay informed about legislative updates that can impact their profitability, such as changes to tax relief on mortgage interest and the introduction of stricter lending criteria. Staying abreast of these developments is essential for landlords to navigate the complexities of buy to let investments successfully. Engaging with professional advisors can further enhance their understanding and compliance with current regulations.

In conclusion, while buy to let mortgages present a valuable opportunity for property investors, they require careful consideration and proactive management. By conducting thorough research, planning finances meticulously, and staying informed about market trends and regulations, landlords can position themselves for success in the competitive UK property market. Ultimately, a strategic approach to buy to let mortgages can lead to rewarding investment experiences and long-term financial benefits.

## Resources for Further Learning

To deepen your understanding of buy to let mortgages and navigate the complexities of property investment in the UK, it is essential to explore a variety of resources. Books dedicated to buy to let investment, property management, and the intricacies of buy to let mortgages provide foundational knowledge. Titles such as "The Complete Guide to Property Investment" and "Buy to Let: The Complete Guide" offer insights into market trends, investment strategies, and the financial implications of rental properties. These resources can help both novice and experienced landlords make informed decisions.

Online platforms and forums also serve as valuable resources for landlords seeking to expand their knowledge. Websites such as Property118 and the Landlord Zone offer a wealth of information ranging from articles to forums where landlords can share experiences and seek advice. Engaging in these communities allows investors to keep abreast of changes in legislation, market conditions, and best practices in property management. Additionally, social media groups focused on property investment can facilitate networking and provide real-time insights.

For those interested in the financial aspects of buy to let, industry reports and market analyses from organisations like the UK Finance and the Royal Institution of Chartered Surveyors are indispensable. These reports provide data on mortgage trends, rental yields, and market forecasts, equipping landlords with the necessary information to make sound investment decisions. Understanding economic indicators, such as interest rates and housing supply, can further inform your investment strategy and enhance your ability to anticipate market shifts.

Educational courses and workshops are also beneficial for landlords looking to refine their skills and knowledge. Institutions offering property management and investment courses can provide formal education on legal obligations, financial management, and property valuation. These programs often include practical elements, such as case studies and simulations, allowing participants to apply their learning in real-world scenarios. Many of these courses are available online, making them accessible regardless of location.

Lastly, consulting with professionals in the buy to let market, such as mortgage brokers, property managers, and legal advisors, can provide critical insights tailored to individual circumstances. These experts can offer personalised advice on navigating the complexities of buy to let mortgages, understanding the regulatory environment, and maximising rental income. Building a network of reliable professionals ensures that landlords are well informed and supported throughout their investment journey.

By leveraging these resources, landlords can enhance their knowledge and increase their chances of success in the competitive buy to let market.

www.ingramcontent.com/pod-product-compliance
Lightning Source LLC
Chambersburg PA
CBHW070157230526
45471CB00002B/698